Night Travels

Written and illustrated by Joe Berger

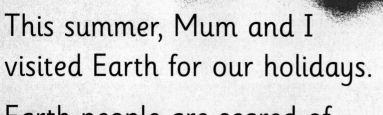

This summer, Mum and I visited Earth for our holidays.

Earth people are scared of aliens, so we travel at night.

Rivers run into the seas. Earth people build villages near rivers.

They call a big village a town.

They call a big town a city.

We visited a city during the day.
It was very busy and very exciting.

We did not want to scare the Earth
people so we dressed up as cats.

We tried lots of food. I liked cake best.

Yum!

We went to a shop filled with toys.

We watched Earth people doing noisy jobs, like digging up roads.

I got chased by a dog. Now I was scared!

I hid up a tree. Now Mum was scared!

Some people called firemen rescued me with a long ladder.

The firemen are not made of fire!

Mum and I went back to our spaceship
to eat more cake.

Earth is a fantastic place to visit.

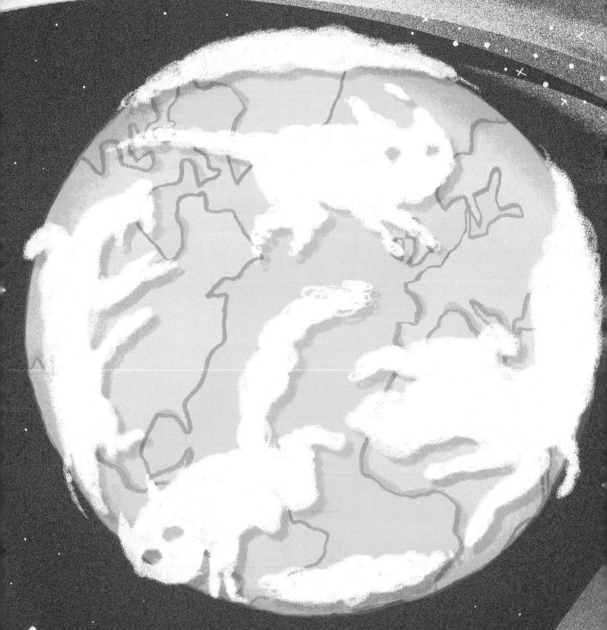

One day I would like to live there,
but only when dogs stop chasing cats.

Talk about the story

Ask your child these questions:

1 Where did the aliens visit during the day?

2 What did the firemen use to rescue the alien?

3 Why did the aliens dress up as cats?

4 Do you think the aliens will come back to live on Earth?

5 Where would you visit if you had a spaceship?

6 Do you prefer going out in the day or at night? Why?

Can your child retell the story in their own words?